SIGNIFICANT IMAGES OF
RAILROADING

From the collections of the Center for Railroad Photography & Art

Scott Lothes
Editor

Jack Holzhueter
Biographical Sketches

Jordan Radke
Archives Manager

Dedication

John Gruber   Art Miller

The Center's directors, officers, and staff members wish to especially thank two people, John Gruber and Arthur Miller, for establishing the Center's photography collections and laying the groundwork for its archiving activities. Gruber is a cofounder and past president of the Center. Preserving significant photographs and bodies of photography, as well as illuminating the lives of their creators, was part of his vision for the Center from its inception in 1997. Miller retired as the archivist at Lake Forest College in 2013 and from the Center's board in 2014. He was one of the Center's original board members and provided a home and resources for its collecting activities at Lake Forest College. The collaborative and mutually beneficial relationship between the Center and the college is part of his legacy. It is thanks in very large part to the efforts of John Gruber and Art Miller that we can bring you these significant images of railroading.

Photographs by Henry A. Koshollek and Steve Crise

With Thanks

Funding for this special publication provided by generous gifts from:

Fred and Dale Springer

Trains magazine

The Candelaria Fund

Bon and Holly French

With additional thanks to these individuals who assisted in preparing this publication and with the Center's archives:

Frank Barry

Jeff Brouws

Norman Carlson

Jim Cascino

Aviva Gellman

Nona Hill

Sharon Hill

David Kahler

Kevin P. Keefe

Frank Keller

John Kelly

Albert O. Louer

Robert Ludwig

Jeff Mast

David Mattoon

Andy Meyer

Ralph Pierce

Polly Rose

Michael P. Schmidt

Joel Skornicka

Brian Solomon

Anne Thomason

Michael R. Valentine

Jim Wrinn

Published by the Center for Railroad Photography & Art
313 Price Place, Suite 13, Madison, Wisconsin 53705-3262
608-251-5785 / info@railphoto-art.org
Copies for sale by U.S. mail or on our website at:
www.railphoto-art.org/store/

The Center's mission is to preserve and present significant images of railroading. Preservation work occurs both in the Center's Madison office and in the:

Archives & Special Collections
Donnelley and Lee Library
Lake Forest College
555 North Sheridan Road
Lake Forest, Illinois 60045-2399
www.lakeforest.edu/library/archives/

The Center achieves its mission through gifts, grants, and collaborations with institutions across the country. See page 76 to learn more. The Center is a 501(c)(3) not-for-profit arts and education organization and financial support is fully tax-deductible.

Design consultants: Phil Hamilton and Jeff Brouws

Contents

Cover: Two streamlined *Hiawatha* passenger trains of the Milwaukee Road at Chicago Union Station, circa 1950, offer striking commentary on industrial design. Leading the train in the background is F7-class 4-6-4 steam locomotive no. 102, designed by Otto Kuhler. One of the famed Skytop Lounge cars, by Brooks Stevens, dominates the foreground. *Wallace W. Abbey*

Foreword

Preservation and presentation of railroading's significant images is the Center for Railroad Photography & Art's foremost mission. Now, for the first time, the Center presents an up-to-date visual summary of its photographic preservation efforts thus far. We are delighted with the results. As you peruse the ninety-three images selected for these seventy-eight pages, I think you will see why.

John Gruber, along with Center cofounders Joel Skornicka and Ralph Pierce, perceived the need for an organization that focused on the visual representation of railroading and its profound impacts on America's—and the world's—history and culture. By necessity, the Center concentrated its early efforts on the more visible work of presenting images—through exhibitions, publications, and conferences. The North American Railway Foundation has provided key support for many of these programs, including funds that gave the Center opportunities to showcase early collecting efforts.

By Scott Lothes
President and Executive Director

The less visible, behind-the-scenes work of preserving imagery and illuminating the lives of its creators has always occupied a place of equal importance. Gruber found a champion in Art Miller, then the archivist of the Archives & Special Collections at the Donnelley and Lee Library of Lake Forest College. The library already had substantial railroad holdings and its staff understood well their importance. Gruber and Miller brokered a collaborative agreement: the Center would collect; the library would organize and house the photographs.

With a safe home secured, Gruber began building the Center's archive. The first major collection entrusted to the Center's care was the photography of Ted Rose, the renowned watercolor artist. More collections followed, including three with tens of thousands of images that now form the backbone of the Center's holdings—the collections of Wallace W. Abbey, John F. Bjorklund, and Fred M. Springer. Acquisition of Abbey's photography led to a *Trains* magazine preservation award, while Springer and his wife Dale made a substantial bequest for preservation and publication. These funds enabled us to achieve the highest preservation standards. We could purchase top-grade, archival storage materials whose compositions do not damage the images they house. And we could engage interns to perform the tedious scanning and data entry required to make these works searchable and shareable.

The Center's archive now contains close to 200,000 photographs. They date from the 1930s to the 2000s, include all six inhabited continents, and encompass a great variety of styles and subject matter. Some collections contain the rich local knowledge of photographers who rarely left their backyards. Other collections provide the wide-ranging observations of continental and intercontinental wanderers. Together, these images document one of the most transformational industries globally, covering the last two centuries of world history. They touch on many aspects of social life and culture, showing passengers, workers, and the parts of the world they occupied and how they made their livings.

These works also say a great deal about their creators—about what was important to them and how they made sense of the world. Many photographers desire invisibility, but none can have it. Sometimes the observer becomes the observed, as in Fred Springer's stunning photograph of African schoolchildren next to the tracks on p. 72, a poignant example of how railroads have fostered cultural interaction and exchange.

The sun rises over the former Erie
Lackawanna electrified tracks at
Dover, New Jersey, on the foggy
morning of May 6, 1981.
John F. Bjorklund

To prepare this publication, I looked at nearly all of our 200,000-some photographs. Doing so has been one of the greatest pleasures of my work for the Center. While seeking out the exceptional, I enjoyed and learned from practically every image I encountered. I realized how each collection has a much wider importance than just the highlights presented here. The experience transformed me from editor to curator—one who makes decisions about collections and through that process acquires accumulated knowledge that will inform their description and refine the ways in which they are used internally and by the public.

Consider David Plowden's collection of railroad publicity photographs (p. 50–53). Most present the staged formality of corporate imagery. Yet Plowden took them in, internalizing their content and meaning, and went on to make some of the most lyrical photographs ever recorded of the end of the steam era in North America. As he learned from them, so can any aspiring photographer learn from any and all of the works housed in our archive.

For all of the informative and educational qualities these photographs possess in total, there are some in each collection that occupy a higher plane. Finding them is a researcher's great reward. These photographs show the railroad's artistic potency. Serious artists initially eschewed the industrial revolution as a subject. Fittingly, a railroad photograph—Alfred Stieglitz's "The Hand of Man" showing a smoking locomotive in the gritty Long Island City yards in 1902—helped bring the art world's attention to industrial subjects. That image also helped elevate the photograph as a medium for fine art. Many of the photographs herein show how the artistic potential of railroad photography has blossomed.

Railroad photography overall is more popular than ever in the twenty-first century, practiced by men—and increasing numbers of women—of all ages throughout the developed world. The swift rise of digital photography has sped the learning and sharing process, while giving all the creative controls of the black-and-white darkroom to the color medium at levels of precision even the best black-and-white printers never could have imagined. Digital photography has also introduced new challenges for long-term storage—archivists still are debating about how best to address unresolved issues of degradation and longevity.

The Center has achieved a critical mass in its preservation efforts as this volume goes to press in early 2015. The groundwork laid by John Gruber and Art Miller, combined with the faith of those photographers and families who have entrusted works to the Center's care, have attracted a highly engaged board of directors and a new level of financial support. Together, our directors and supporters have enabled the Center to begin strategically planning how best to address the overall preservation needs of railroad imagery. Recent, major gifts by the Candelaria Fund and by Bon and Holly French have enabled the Center to hire a full-time archives manager in Madison and secure a long-term agreement with Lake Forest College, where new archivist Anne Thomason continues to champion railroad photography.

The Center's board is now working to establish an endowment to ensure steady funding for all programs, including archiving. The board has already created an acquisitions and collections committee, chaired by Jeff Brouws, which has developed a policy to guide current and future work on collections. Millions more railroad photographs will need new homes in the coming years and decades, and the Center hopes to be a home for many of them.

Chicago & North Western's depot
and freight office in Watertown,
Wisconsin, in the 1970s.
Glenn Oestreich

Wallace W. Abbey Collection

Wallace W. "Wally" Abbey was a rarity among railroad photographers because he was both a railroad industry insider and an avid and accomplished railroad photographer. His years as a railroad public relations figure gave him access to locations most rail photographers only dream about. And some of the railroad events he covered were among the most historic of the last half of the twentieth century.

The Abbey Collection's roughly 35,000 images cover the 1940s into the 2000s, and they amply illustrate the transition from steam to diesel, one of Abbey's favorite topics. Abbey's own twenty-five favorites—he selected them in 2004—demonstrate that he belonged to the army of railfans that laments steam's demise. The collection is especially strong for 1950–1954, the years he worked as an associate editor at *Trains* magazine, a job that required him to make judgments about pictures every day. That experience possibly led to his making tough judgments about his own work and to refining his artist's eye, a skill he put to highly visible use in 1962 when he designed the Soo Line's red and light-gray color scheme.

Wally Abbey (1927–2014) was born to Wallace W. and Margaret Abbey and grew up in Evanston, Illinois. His father was a copy editor for the *Chicago Tribune*, and he had grandparents who lived in Cherryvale, Kansas, a small town in southeast Kansas with a railroad background. (The Kansas City, Lawrence & Southern Kansas Railroad platted Cherryvale in 1871.) When Abbey visited there in 1940, a year before the U.S. involvement in World War II, he got hooked on railroad photography. Two important lines crossed in Cherryvale—the Frisco and Santa Fe—with an interurban line, the Union Traction Company, only an eighth of a mile from the crossing. (Using interurban connections, you could ride electric passenger trains from Cherryvale north to St. Louis and south to Little Rock.)

With a population of only 3,000 during Abbey's boyhood, Cherryvale's most alluring attraction was assuredly the railroad. Young Abbey chose to stand trackside with a new camera, awaiting the trains just as railroad photographers always have. He made his first railroad image that year and continued during World War II (1941–1945) when film and printing paper were sometimes hard to find. During the school year in Evanston he hung out with other youthful railfans, and they made frequent trips a few miles south to railroad destinations in Chicago—engine terminals, stations, and yards. There he fell in love with the Santa Fe and the Chicago & North Western, and in the summer of 1944 the Santa Fe gave him a seasonal job in the diesel repair shop.

At war's end, he entered the University of Kansas in Lawrence as a journalism student, taking his camera with him. Beginning in 1949 he wrote articles for *Trains*, and he joined the magazine's staff in 1950 after college graduation. He worked there until 1954, and then moved into railroad public relations work: Association of Western Railways (1954–1956), *Railway Age* (1956–1959), Soo Line (1959–1970), independent consultant (1970–1975), Milwaukee Road (1975–1980), Trailer Train (1980–1982), and for the American Association of Railroads at its test center in Pueblo, Colorado (1982–1991).

While with the Milwaukee Road, Abbey documented the demise of the line's western division pictorially, showing the shocking physical deterioration of the line that presaged the railroad's collapse. He had no formal training as a photographer, but credited the Soo Line's

graphic design firm, Merlin Krupp, for influencing his work. He also learned from personal experimentation, he said. In 2003 he received a lifetime photographic achievement award from the Railway & Locomotive Historical Society.

Abbey's publications are equally notable. The *Trains* index credits him with sixty-three articles, fifteen of them for a series of articles about notable railroad engineering feats. The worldwide online library catalog, WorldCat, lists seven works, appearing in 119 different libraries. His most prominent publication is *The Little Jewel: Soo Line Railroad Company and the Locomotives That Make It Go* of 1984, held by sixty-two libraries around the world. Extended profiles about Abbey and his career appear in *Classic Trains*, Summer 2010, pages 36–45; and *Trains*, August 2012, pages 42–47.

In 2010 Abbey, his wife Martha, and his daughters Mary "Maggie" Abbey and Martha Abbey Miller donated his railroad photography to the Center. Both Wally and his wife have died since then. Geographically, the collection focuses on the upper Midwest and especially Chicago and the Twin Cities, along with Kansas, Colorado, and a smattering from both coasts. The most-featured railroads are the Soo Line, Milwaukee Road, and Santa Fe, but many others are included. Passenger trains, stations, shops, and interlocking towers were among Abbey's favorite subjects. With an insider's knowledge and an artist's eye, he created a sweeping yet intimate portrayal of American railroading from its zenith during World War II, through the dark decades that followed, and into its revival.

Baltimore & Ohio passenger trains meet at Deshler, Ohio, on September 23, 1952.

　　Wallace W. Abbey Collection

Left: An eastbound Santa Fe freight train behind 2-8-2 no. 4070 crosses the Illinois River on its way out of Chillicothe, Illinois, in 1946.

Below: An eastbound Union Pacific freight train has just exited one of the Hermosa tunnels on Wyoming's Sherman Hill on August 17, 1957. Road power is 4-8-8-4 "Big Boy" no. 4019, assisted by 4-8-4 no. 829 as a headend helper. The engines are working hard as they climb toward the Continental Divide.

Just south of Chicago's La Salle
Street Station on August 21, 1950,
an inbound Rock Island train meets
an outbound New York Central train
led by E7A no. 4031 while an NYC
switcher works the yard in the background. Abbey photographed from
the Roosevelt Road overpass.

In 1952, Chicago & North Western 4-6-2 no. 514 rides the turntable at the road's 40th Street terminal, located along Kinzie Street between Pulaski Road and Kilbourn Avenue, which serviced engines for the C&NW's extensive Chicago-area commuter serivce.

Right: Under the large train shed of Chicago's Dearborn Station on February 2, 1952, the engineer of a Wabash passenger train stands next to his locomotive, 4-6-4 no. 702.

Below: On June 3, 1951, the Great Northern's new "Mid Century" *Empire Builder* is being prepared for its inaugural run at Chicago's 14th Street yards. The Chicago, Burlington & Quincy Railroad handled the train between Chicago and Minneapolis, and two of its E8A diesel locomotives are powering the GN's brand-new streamlined passenger cars. Many of Abbey's Chicago views capture the city's internationally famous and evolving skyline as an important by-product of his documenting both quotidian operations and milestones of railroading.

Eastbound Pennsylvania Railroad passenger train behind K4-class steam locomotive no. 5497 crossing the Chicago River at Chicago's 21st Street Tower in October 1950. The bridge, located just south of Union Station, is down to allow the train's passage. In its raised position, the bridge permitted boats to travel this industrial stretch of the river, whose flow had been reversed fifty years earlier so that it did not empty into Lake Michigan, but rather became a tributary of the Mississippi. The feat was an engineering marvel equal to railroading's many engineering marvels.

Left: At Joliet, Illinois, a Santa Fe freight train waits in the background while a Rock Island train crosses in front at that city's Union Station on October 14, 1951.

Below, left: At Crystal, Minnesota, a northwest suburb of Minneapolis, a Soo Line freight train crosses in front of a waiting Great Northern train on April 10, 1961. Abbey, who was working for the Soo Line at the time, used the cars and couplers of the Soo Line train to frame the distant GN locomotive.

Opposite: Union Pacific steam locomotives congregate inside the roundhouse at Council Bluffs, Iowa, on February 4, 1957. At left is 2-8-2 no. 2242, which was retired later that year. Thanks to the ventilation hoods over every stall, this roundhouse stayed cleaner than earlier ones.

Wallace W. Abbey Collection

Left: In a May 1961 test run, three General Motors demonstrator GP20 diesel locomotives lead an eastbound Soo Line freight train across the spectacular High Bridge over the St. Croix River at Somerset, Wisconsin.

Right: Inspecting the Milwaukee Road along the Jefferson River near Sappington, Montana, on October 9, 1979. Federal bankruptcy Trustee Richard B. Ogilvie, a former Illinois governor, wanted to make personally sure of his abandonment recommendation. The inspection party traveled east from Seattle and Tacoma to Roundup, Montana, mostly on the Milwaukee Road route using a Chevy Suburban outfitted as a hi-rail vehicle (flanged wheels as well as rubber tires). The Northern Pacific tracks across the river are still used by Montana Rail Link. Compare this to John Bjorklund's view on p. 26.

Opposite: At the summit of Cajon Pass in California, a westbound Santa Fe freight train meets Union Pacific's eastbound *City of Los Angeles* on April 28, 1970. Barely a year remains for the *City*, which was discontinued with the creation of Amtrak on May 1, 1971.

John F. Bjorklund Collection

John Bjorklund's father, Walter, a division engineer for the Northern Pacific Railway, probably introduced his son to railroading before the boy could walk or talk. John grew up absorbing, learning, and enjoying vast stretches of the Northern Pacific in the western states. He started with Tacoma, Washington, where he was born to Barbara and Walter Bjorklund in 1939. Tacoma sits at the southern extremity of Puget Sound, about thirty miles south of central Seattle, and it abounds with rail and maritime facilities. In addition to the NP, the Milwaukee Road, the Great Northern and the Union Pacific also served the city. Then the family moved to Billings in south-central Montana on the Yellowstone River, where John attended elementary school and added the Chicago, Burlington & Quincy to his list of hometown lines. Next came St. Paul, Minnesota, the head of navigation on the Mississippi. There John attended high school and college—the University of Minnesota's St. Paul campus, the "real" U of M in his opinion, not the larger campus in Minneapolis. In St. Paul he could add the Chicago & North Western, Chicago Great Western, Soo Line, and Minneapolis & St. Louis to the list of lines he grew up with.

Of all these railroads, Bjorklund (1939–2005) remained faithful to the Northern Pacific, his principal love, but shared his affections with its successor, the Burlington Northern, as well as the Milwaukee Road and—out of left field—the Erie Lackawanna. He also fancied big passenger trains, like the NP's flagship *North Coast Limited.*

After college, he served two years in the U.S. Army. He was stationed at Fort Knox, Kentucky, where he conducted psychological tests for soldiers. Following his discharge in 1965, he returned to St. Paul and found a job with the Ford Motor Company. A few years later, Ford transferred him to Detroit, and he remained in that area until his death in 2005. Bjorklund had retired in 1999, having achieved corporate officer status as a traffic analyst, coordinating the transportation of auto body parts and finished automobiles by rail and truck. Through these professional contacts, as well as through his interest in rail photography, he developed many railroad-based friendships.

It is safe to say that railfans generally do not favor classical music and opera. But Bjorklund was an exception. He collected recordings and attended live performances. And he combined his two interests—music and railroading—in several slide shows of railroad photographs set to classical music, finding appropriate instrumental and vocal pieces for each photographic sequence.

Most photographers commonly remember details about many images they have made. Bjorklund's memory, however, vastly surpassed the customary. Friends said he was "a walking hard drive" for his recall of details, dates, and locations. Yet he did not rely on memory alone. Every single one of his slides includes, at a minimum, location and date.

Bjorklund took up railroad photography in the late 1960s. He came to love signals, signal towers, and stations, frequently photographing them or using them as compositional elements. His favorite subject by far was semaphores, which he called "blades." In all his photography, he made a point of covering disappearing aspects of railroading before they vanished altogether. He photographed much of Canada and the U.S. In the last ten years of his life, his most frequent photographic companions were Bob Kessler and Jim Koglin.

Friends dubbed them "The Group of Three." Other partners came from the Detroit Tuesday Night Slide Club, whose members met on Tuesdays to share their photographs. Bjorklund's other photography companions from the club included Emery Gulash, Doug Harrop, Jeff Mast, Mike Schafer, and Jim Thomas.

In the 1980s Bjorklund commissioned a large painting by Larry Fisher which derived from one of his favorite photographs from his own body of work (opposite, above). The painting shows the Milwaukee Road's *Olympian Hiawatha* with electric boxcab E14 overtaking a westbound NP freight headed by Z6 Challenger steam locomotive no. 5117. The photograph (right) depicts everyday freight trains of the diesel era.

In 1990, Bjorklund was married, and his wife, Rose, survived him. In 2011 she presented his collection of 55,000 color slides to the Center. The Center's Michael R. Valentine and Jeff Mast helped significantly with arranging the acquisition, and Mast compiled a biography on which this sketch is based. Bjorklund's photography covers much of North America and dates between the late 1960s and early 2000s—known as the "Kodachrome Era" of railroad photography for the film that became a staple of railroad photographers nationwide due to its color rendition and longevity. For the strengths of its organization, subject matter, and compositions, the Bjorklund Collection is among the best of its age.

Lehigh Valley freight train led by Alco C628 no. 631 passing under the Erie Lackawanna's Starrucca Viaduct in Lanesboro, Pennsylvania, on July 22, 1975. Both railroads became part of Conrail in the following year, and before the end of the decade, the LV tracks had been abandoned. The railroad atop the viaduct survives and today is part of the New York, Susquehanna & Western.

Above: A Burlington Northern freight train on the former Northern Pacific Railroad, led by GP9 no. 1712, running along the parallel Milwaukee Road, whose SD40-2 no. 142 is in the siding at Iris, Montana, on July 10, 1979. The Milwaukee Road was electrified through here until 1974; the wires are gone but the poles remain. The Milwaukee tracks were abandoned the following year, but the Northern Pacific line survives as part of the Montana Rail Link.

Left: Erie Lackawanna GP35 no. 2570 leads a westbound freight train past the tower and semaphore signal at North Judson, Indiana, on March 28, 1976.

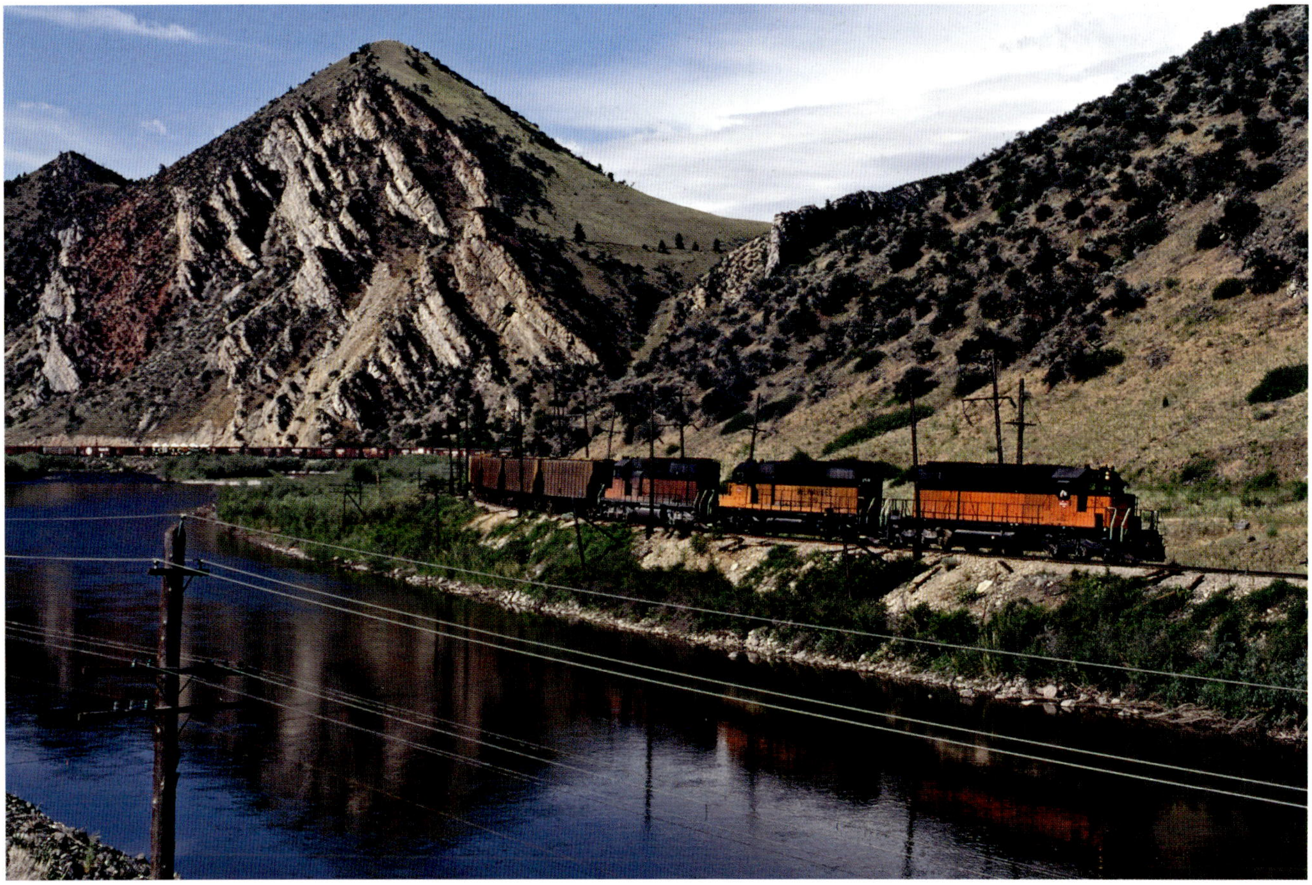

Above: John Bjorklund grew up in the northwest and returned almost every summer to photograph its railroads. The Milwaukee Road was one of his favorites, and here westbound freight train no. 201 is running along the Jefferson River near Jefferson Island, Montana, on July 8, 1979. Compare this to Wallace Abbey's view on p. 21.

Right: Milwaukee Road "Little Joe" electric motor no. E21 leading a freight train through Loweth, Montana, on July 7, 1973. The Milwaukee Road ended its electric operations the following year.

Left: Bjorklund made special efforts to photograph branch lines as well as main lines, and he covered many of the Soo Line's branches in North Dakota. In this view, he framed GP38-2 no. 4401 with playground equipment while it led a short freight train through the town of Baldwin on July 7, 1980. Bjorklund stretched to include a crossbuck warning sign at far left.

Below: Bjorklund commenced his photography of railroads in the mid-1960s while working for Ford in St. Paul, Minnesota. In one of his earliest views, Chicago, Burlington & Qunicy train no. 21, the *Morning Zephyr* from Chicago, is arriving in Minneapolis and crossing the Great Northern's Stone Arch Bridge over the Mississippi River in April 1966. The bridge is now a pedestrian and bike path.

John F. Bjorklund Collection

Three Sunsets

Left: Semaphores guard the Conrail main line at Quincy, Ohio, at sunset on March 15, 1980.

Below: Canadian National eastbound freight train carrying automobiles at Hyde Park, Ontario, as the sun sets on February 4, 1978.

Opposite: Detroit, Toledo & Ironton northbound freight train crossing the Great Miami River in Quincy, Ohio, on March 22, 1980.

Ken Burbach Collection

Burbach Collection Overview
Gift of Ken Burbach
2,000 color slides
1960s to 1980s
Upper Midwest

The Center's headquarters are in Madison, Wisconsin, and it is only natural that Wisconsin collections find their way into the Center's archives more readily than collections created by photographers from other states. But Burbach's photography is far from Wisconsin-bound. It ranges around the Midwest and emphasizes the railroad environment for use in Burbach's model railroad work—his real love.

Burbach has put most of his railfan effort into two model railroads, built on two levels and based in part on his own photographs. The first, occupying the lower level, consists of Lionel trains that he lets his grandchildren play with. The second is HO-scale and on the upper level, featuring his favorite Santa Fe line, and, he commands, "Kids, don't touch it."

Burbach has seldom left the house without a camera since he was a boy. He was born in Richland Center in southwest Wisconsin in 1937, a town served only by a branch line of the Milwaukee Road, now abandoned. About 1939, the family moved some fifty miles southwest to Lancaster, served by the Chicago & North Western, and very near the end of the C&NW line from Madison to the east. Trains were not especially frequent, but it helped Ken that the Burbach house was only a block or two from the tracks and a three-stall roundhouse. It also helped that World War II was underway and that the postwar boom occurred when Ken was a boy so Lancaster train traffic was at its peak. The station agent befriended Ken, and he got to know crew members as well. He would ride his bicycle to the station, and the crew often gave him rides on their train.

Besides the daily attraction of local freight and passenger trains, Ken occasionally was treated to long-distance trips to Southern California, where his mother had relatives. She ran a dress shop in Lancaster, and when business was good, or about every two years, the family enjoyed a trip on the Santa Fe's *Super Chief*. In off years, they traveled on the less-expensive *El Capitan*. The combination of personal travel and local exposure hooked Ken.

In 1949 the Burbach family moved a hundred miles northeast to Portage, Wisconsin, a Milwaukee Road town on the main line with lots of activity compared to Lancaster. Friends of Burbach's father worked for the railroad, and they fostered Ken's interests.

Burbach's high school graduation occurred during the Korean War, and he served three years in the Army there, after which he attended Carroll College (now Carroll University) in Waukesha, Wisconsin, just west of Milwaukee. Then he taught history at the high school in New Berlin, Wisconsin, a southwest Milwaukee suburb that puts the accent in Berlin on the first syllable. He ended his professional career working in the Madison area for a private publishing firm, the Bureau of National Affairs in Washington, DC.

All along, he kept his camera at hand. His wife, he admits, was "not a big railfan," but she enjoys the occasional long-distance train trip. Together, they have ridden the *Canadian* across Canada, the *Orient Express* to Istanbul, and the *Blue Train* of South Africa. Burbach donated some two thousand color slides to the Center, and, as he suggests, their strength can be found in infrastructure and equipment, covering the 1960s to the 1980s.

Left: Soo Line GP38-2 no. 4403 at the turntable in front of the railroad's roundhouse in Marquette, Michigan, in February 1987. The engine facility was demolished ten years later and sold to the city in 2001.

Below: This tangle of tracks is made by three railroads at aptly named Grand Crossing Tower in La Crosse, Wisconsin. This 1982 view from the tower looks west down the double-track main line of the Milwaukee Road toward the distant bluffs of the Mississippi River. At bottom is the Chicago, Burlington & Quincy's main line between Chicago and the Twin Cities. Crossing both on a diagonal is the "city line" of the Chicago & North Western (since abandoned). The tower was closed in 1991 and moved to a park in La Crosse.

The coaling tower in Dekalb, Illinois, is silhouetted against an overcast sky in May 1980, in this view looking east on the Chicago & North Western main line to Chicago. Structures were among Burbach's primary rail photography subjects, in part to serve as reference material for his model railroads.

Perry Frank Johnson Collection

The first two photographs in Frank Johnson's set of forty-one railroad albums were taken not by Johnson himself but by his wife, Dorothea Nance Johnson, in the spring of 1942. (In some of his earliest notebooks from the 1930s he calls himself Frank, not Perry.) Mrs. Johnson intended them as a nudge to her husband to take up photography "because," as he captioned the second image, "he was crazy about trains." So crazy, in fact, that in the late 1930s he had spent tedious hours creating lists of cars on freight trains near where he lived—no pictures, just exhaustive lists, often written on the backs of discarded mimeographed announcements for activities at the Indianapolis YMCA.

Then World War II and Army service at the headquarters of an armored division in Europe intervened in Johnson's life from 1942 through 1945. But on March 1, 1946, he began his years-long rail-photography avocation, writing, "One has to start somewhere if he is to take action pictures of railroad subjects, and after putting it off for a while I started here—on 11th St. in Michigan City, Indiana," where he was working for the YMCA.

Johnson (1913–2007) majored in biology for his bachelor's degree and had obviously developed a scientist's love for categorizing and description—taxonomy. He applied this training to railroads and the images he took, largely in northern Indiana, in and around Michigan City, and in northeastern Ohio, in and around Elyria, where he took another YMCA job in 1948. The early albums are meticulously organized, each image printed personally by Johnson and accompanied by typewritten descriptions. Later, he reduced the captioning, perhaps because it was better to put photographs in albums without writing a paragraph about each image than to let the images pile up unmounted.

Johnson did not discriminate among steam, electric, and diesel. He shot what he saw locally, sometimes with people in the images. His first photograph was of a Chicago South Shore & South Bend freight train, with an animated engineer leaning out of the cab. His last images were made in the late 1950s. Railroad historian Brian Solomon finds Johnson's circumscribed universe a plus for researchers. He calls the albums "a valuable documentary record of everyday railroading," which illustrates "the crucial time period … when America's railroads were making the transition from steam to diesel. … He…didn't shy away from photographing diesels at a time when many serious photographers shunned them."

Professionally Johnson worked for the Elyria Y's boys program through 1961, and he ran its summer camp's nature museum and classes. From the Y he moved to the Lorain County park system as a naturalist and newsletter editor. He assisted in founding the local Audubon chapter, and he edited its newsletter, too. The park system has named a visitor center for him.

Frank Johnson retired in 1984. In 2009 his widow donated his railroad photographs to the Center—ensuring that the very work she encouraged him to produce would be safe and available for the future.

Opposite: New York Central 4-6-4 J1-class steam locomotive no. 5260 charging through Elyria, Ohio, with eastbound train no. 78 on December 29, 1946. The train is passing the Ridge Tool Company and the engine is taking water "on the fly" from a track pan located between the rails, evidenced by the cloud of spray enveloping the tender.

Johnson Collection Overview
Gift of Dorothea Nance Johnson
Forty-one albums of B&W prints
1940s and 1950s
Indiana, Ohio, Illinois, and California

Top: Chicago South Shore & South Bend "motors" nos. 1002 and 1014 lead a twelve-car "extra" freight train down Eleventh Street at Franklin Street in Michigan City, Indiana, at 5:47 p.m. on July 11, 1947.

Middle: Michigan City, Indiana, on New Year's Day in 1947, as seen from the top of a dune next to Trail Creek. The view is looking west down the New York Central's main line, where a westbound freight train with 2-8-2 no. 2027 and twenty-one cars is departing.

Bottom: An A-B set of Alco diesels (nos. 1089 and 3317) leads a ninety-three-car westbound freight train on the New York Central's main line at Amherst, Ohio, on June 14, 1956. The view is from the Quarry Road overpass, a favorite location for photographer Johnson.

Left: Seen from the seventeenth floor of the YMCA Hotel in Chicago is this northbound Chicago North Shore local train at Eighth Street on June 9, 1946. Johnson worked for the "Y" and put his access to good use for this overhead vantage, showing the railroad in the context of the dense urban environment it served.

Below: Baltimore & Ohio Chicago Terminal 0-8-0 steam locomotive no. 767 switching Pullman cars on May 13, 1950, as seen from Chicago's Roosevelt Road overpass.

Leo King Collection

The world of transportation was both a lifelong preoccupation and occupation of Leo King (1938–2011). He grew up in Providence, Rhode Island, and developed an avid interest in trains while in grammar school. He freely admitted he favored field work about trains—hooky—over regular classroom attendance by the time he was eight years old, well before the onset of teenage rebelliousness.

In his youth King particularly photographed trains at Providence's mile-long East Side Tunnel (with portals under Benefit and Gano Streets). The city's Union Station, he said, was nearly a home away from home. Early in his railfan life, he discovered the former New England Railfan Association and regularly took advantage of its excursions, other picture-making opportunities, and exposure to railroad knowledge—something never taught in his schoolrooms. Despite his lack of affinity for formal education, along the way he earned a bachelor of arts degree.

King had several careers and worked in transportation in all of them. He served in the Air Force and learned to fly light planes like Cessna 172s, Piper Cherokees, and Warriors. He spent a few years as a bridge operator on the Mystic River (a seven-mile-long stream in the Boston area), the Niantic River (the "Nan" in eastern Connecticut with a bascule railroad bridge), and Old Lyme Drawbridge on the Connecticut River, the last crossing before the river flows into Long Island Sound. Beginning in 1988, King worked for Amtrak on the Northeast Corridor between Boston and New Haven as a train director and block operator.

For thirty years he worked as an editor and writer, "particularly in transportation topics," as he put it. He contributed articles to *Railfan & Railroad*, *RailNews*, and *Passenger Train Journal*. Professionally he also worked in radio as an anchor and reporter for various Rhode Island radio stations. Toward the end of his life, he edited a weekly online magazine called *Destination: Freedom*, published by the National Corridors Initiative.

Wherever he lived and worked, King photographed avidly, notably including the years he served in Alaska with the Air Force. In 1972, he won first place for a black-and-white print in the National Model Railroading Association's "Evergreen Convention," sponsored by the Pacific Northwest Region of the association. He retired to Middleburg, Florida, near Jacksonville, in 2002, and maintained his interest in writing about railroads and making railroad photographs as long as he was physically able.

King donated his photography collection in 2006. It consists of about 1,200 images and includes detailed notebooks about them. Particular strengths of the collection are its coverage of the New Haven Railroad during the 1950s (black and white) and of the Alaska Railroad during the 1970s (color and black and white).

Opposite: Northbound Alaska Railroad passenger train in the early 1970s running along Turnagain Arm en route to Anchorage behind an A-B-B-A set of F7 locomotives.

King Collection Overview
Gift of Leo King
1,000 B&W negatives
200 color transparencies
1940s to 1990s
United States, especially Alaska and New England

Alaska Railroaders in the 1970s

Right: Robert W. Davison handles paperwork at the Anchorage yard.

Below, left: Gene Owens rides a boxcar during switching moves in the Anchorage yard.

Below, right: Kenny Fuller at the controls of the Whittier Shuttle.

Special thanks to Frank Keller for finding the identifies of these railroaders, whose names originally went unrecorded.

Left: New Haven caboose C-667 and an Alco diesel switcher lead a local freight train into Providence, Rhode Island's East Side Tunnel about 1950. The tunnel was one of King's favorite photography locations in his hometown. He made this 127-format photograph when he was only about twelve years old.

Below: New Haven DL109 no. 0729 at the railroad's Charles Street Roundhouse in Providence, Rhode Island, in the late 1950s. As a teenager, King began using a 616-format camera, a step up for him.

Harold O. Lewis Collection

Harold O. "Hal" Lewis's late father, a professor of history, launched Hal into photography in the late 1940s by giving him a camera when he was a high school junior. Lewis is a 1953 aeronautical engineering graduate of Purdue University in West Lafayette, Indiana, and a highly successful, now retired engineer for Boeing and Lockheed. He has photographed railroads for more than sixty years.

His biography sounds like that of the fairly common variety of railroad enthusiast who is a professional engineer and who just happens to come from an academic background. The only wrinkle is that Hal Lewis is African American, a segment of the U.S. population under-represented not only in academe but also among railfans and railroad photographers.

Lewis's father, the senior Harold O. Lewis, taught at Howard University in Washington, DC, one of the nation's most distinguished African American institutions where being a European American places you in the minority. His father was recruited by the Franklin D. Roosevelt administration to work on top-secret German translation projects during World War II—another startlingly rare occurrence in the history of America's black community. When the younger Lewis asked his father about his World War II work, he was told "I can't tell you." When his own children asked him about his under-wraps Lockheed work, Lewis had to tell them, too, "I can't tell you."

Lewis came into his own as a railfan and photographer at Purdue. He made friends with New York Central engine crews who saw him taking pictures. "I began to get cab rides and I was soon taught to fire," which he did rather than attend Purdue's football and basketball games—although "I did go out for baseball." He particularly liked photographing Nickel Plate and New York Central trains as they plied the one percent grade westbound out of the Wabash River valley near Purdue. Hal's "work" as a fireman was known to railroad officials, but they looked the other way. Such an arrangement would be unthinkable today.

While employed in Seattle by Boeing from 1953 to 1958, Lewis photographed steam operations over the border in western British Columbia—on both the Canadian National and Canadian Pacific. In 1958 an offer from Lockheed let Lewis and his wife and son escape "the long rainy winters in Seattle" and move to Sunnyvale, California, where they added a daughter to the family.

In southern California Lewis liked photographing steam on the Southern Pacific, which was quickly phasing it out. He particularly captured the narrow-gauge, lumber-hauling legend in the Sierra foothills, the Westside Lumber Company. He took railfan trips to South America, especially to Argentina and Brazil. And from time to time he returned to Canada for railfan vacations. Following his 1989 retirement, he took on a more active role in railfan organizations, and he was a central figure in planning the 1992 national convention of the National Railway Historical Society.

Hal Lewis donated more than two hundred black-and-white negatives to the Center in 2011, as well as several hundred color slides. Their importance to the industrial history of steam operations in North America is self-explanatory. Their importance to the social history of the railfan community cannot be overestimated.

Opposite: New York Central 2-8-2 no. 1570 teams up with a 4-8-2 to lift a heavy westbound freight train out of the Wabash River valley in West Lafayette, Indiana, circa 1950.

Lewis Collection Overview
Gift of Harold O. Lewis
200 B&W negatives
500 color slides
1950s to 1990s
Unitied States, Canada, and Mexico, especially Indiana and California

Left: West Side Lumber Company three-foot gauge Shay no. 9 leading a loaded log train toward the sawmill at Tuolumne, California, circa 1960.

Below, left: Two National Railway of Mexico narrow-guage 2-8-0s lead a heavy freight train in central Mexico in the 1960s.

Opposite, above: New York Central J-1 4-6-4 no. 5333 storming up the one percent grade out of the Wabash River valley near West Lafayette, Indiana, with a westbound train of heavyweight passenger cars on a cold winter day circa 1950. The J-1 "Hudson" was the photographer's favorite locomotive.

Opposite, below: While Hal Lewis strongly favored steam, fans of early diesels can be grateful he made an exception for this circa 1950 view of a Baltimore & Ohio passenger train departing Washington, DC, behind E6A no. 61. One of Washington Terminal's Alco RS1s can be seen switching passenger cars in the coach yards behind the train, while the United States Capitol building is visible in the background at far right.

Glenn Oestreich Collection

The steam engine fascinated Glenn Oestreich (1952–2009), a lifelong resident of the city of Watertown, Wisconsin. He liked steam engines whether they were attached to a model, an antique tractor, or a locomotive. Around the time he was graduated from Watertown High School in 1970, he added photography to his list of hobbies, and he made photographs avidly well into the 2000s.

Oestreich died at the age of fifty-six in 2009. A year later his surviving parents, Shirley and Del Oestreich, selected the Center to receive many of his railroad images, including about two thousand black-and-white prints (mostly 5x7s and 8x10s), several thousand black-and-white negatives (both 35mm and medium format), and about one thousand color slides. Oestreich focused on his home region—Wisconsin and other parts of the Upper Midwest—and on convenient railroads, including the Chicago & North Western, Milwaukee Road, Soo Line, Burlington Northern, and several regional and short lines.

Oestreich was sufficiently passionate about photography to have taken two courses on the subject when he attended the University of Wisconsin-La Crosse. He learned darkroom techniques there and made prints of high technical quality.

Professionally, Oestreich worked at one of the many immense food-processing plants operated by Seneca Foods around the United States. This one is in tiny Clyman, Wisconsin, a village of 800 a few miles north of Watertown in a highly productive agricultural area. The Clyman plant produces mostly canned and bottled vegetables and vegetable products under various brand names.

Oestreich's avocational life was rich and involved. He served on the board of the Dodge County Antique Power Club and handled its publicity; he also was a member of the Grellton Flywheelers. He assisted in restoring antique tractors and engines—a commonplace hobby throughout much of the agricultural Midwest and one with obvious links to railroading and railroad photography.

Right: Three varieties of Chicago & North Western Alcos at the engine terminal in Escabana, Michigan, on a May evening in 1984. At left is high-nose C628 no. 6720, in the middle is RS32 no. 4240, and C425 no. 4257 is at right. The photograph was taken with lighting provided by the the C&NW Historical Society as part of their annual meeting.

Below: Westbound Milwaukee Road freight train crossing a branch of the Chicago & North Western in Watertown, Wisconsin, on May 2, 1976. Leading the train is Milwaukee Road no. 1, an FP45 diesel locomotive. The Milwaukee Road depot, at left, was built in 1926 and closed in 1984; it was later demolished.

Glenn Oestreich Collection

Above: Chicago & North Western local freight train switching industries around the Port of Milwaukee on June 5, 1975. The view is from the operator's shanty on the drawbridge over the Kinnikinnic River.

Left: Unidentified Chicago & North Western operator inside Clyman Junction (Wisconsin) tower in the 1970s. The "pistol grip" levers at right controlled track switches and signals in the area, including an at-grade crossing of the C&NW's main line across Wisconsin and a north-south branch line. The tower was since closed and demolished.

David Plowden Collection of Railroad Publicity Photographs

David Plowden of Winnetka, Illinois, is one of the world's leading photographers of American landscapes and built environments, having portrayed half a century of sweeping changes. Railroads and especially steam locomotives were his first subjects, and railfans everywhere covet those photographs, which he began making more than sixty years ago. He is donating his personal photographic archive to Yale University in New Haven, Connecticut. But he has already donated to the Center a collection of 145 railroad publicity photographs made by other photographers in the 1930s, '40s, and '50s. As a child and a young man, he wrote to many railroads requesting information about their steam locomotives, and many responded by sending him black and white prints. He found them useful research tools for making his own, now famous photographs of steam locomotives.

Railroad publicity photographs are often confused with "real-time" photographs. The difference is that the railroads paid for the publicity photographs and carefully orchestrated them. Locomotives and entire trains were staged in optimal locations. Passengers and crew members in publicity shots were often actual employees of the railroad, not models, and everything about the photographs looks too tidy and organized to be "real." Every napkin and water glass is in place; every uniform is starched and pressed to perfection. Unlike photographs made by independent railroad photographers, these publicity images were not caught on the fly by a photographer, nor were they shot from less-than-ideal vantage points. They often lack the technical finesse and exquisite lighting that an art photographer brings to making an image. But the publicity images were intended to be good for business. For an art photographer like Plowden, publicity photographs are useful reference tools, providing specific details about equipment or operations. Publicity photographs help photographers know what to look for, even a photographer as accomplished as David Plowden.

Above: Electric, diesel, and steam locomotives of the Great Northern Railway. After being graduated from Yale, David Plowden worked for the Great Northern as an assistant to the trainmaster in Willmar, Minnesota, in 1955–1956 where he made some of his first railroad photographs. This Great Northern Railway photograph was made by Riehle Studios from St. Paul, Minnesota.

Right: Five streamlined Santa Fe passenger trains in Chicago, circa 1938. Steam locomotive no. 3460, a 4-6-4, is flanked by four of the Electro-Motive Corporation's E1 diesel-electric locomotives.
Santa Fe Railway

Four sets of Erie diesel-electrics—
Alco FAs on the two middle tracks
flanked by General Motors Electro-
Motive Division E8s on the left and
FTs on the right—were posed for the
company photographer at the shops
in Hornell, New York, circa 1953.
Erie Railroad

Ted Rose Collection

Rose Collection Overview
On deposit from Polly Rose
4,400 B&W prints and negatives
1950s and 1960s
Late steam-era in the midwestern United States, Mexico, the Canadian Prairies, and Guatemala

Watercolors by Ted Rose (1940–2002) stand in the first rank of twentieth-century American railroad art. In 1999, the U.S. Postal Service selected him to paint five locomotives for the "All Aboard" stamp series, and Amtrak picked him as the artist for its 1997, 1998, and 1999 calendars. Serious collectors of railroad art keenly desire works by Ted Rose. Although he painted as a young man and as an art major in college, financial necessity and regular, daily employment led him to neglect this element of his artistic passion until 1983. He then resumed painting and continued until shortly before his death, producing more than a thousand works in less than twenty years, each of them evocative of railroading more than a slavish depiction of it. To achieve these works, Rose wrote that he relied on photographs, not an artist's sketchbook, to achieve authenticity. This was hardly a cheat. Artists from the Renaissance forward to the second quarter of the nineteenth century used the camera obscura to cameras to cast real outlines on their canvases.

What is far less known about Rose's art is his photography. Railroads and making pictures of them captured his imagination when he was in his teens. He was a Milwaukeean by birth (his father was an architect who designed industrial buildings and spaces), and Milwaukee was principally an industrial city. So opportunities abounded there for railroad photography, and Chicago's rail riches—and rail connections to the rest of the nation and continent—were only ninety miles south.

Rose began making railroad pictures when he was fifteen or sixteen; he stopped when he was twenty-two. During those years he photographed the demise of steam and searched out existing steam operations in the U.S., Canada, Mexico, and Guatemala. On these journeys he not only learned about capturing light in just the right way to create an artistically worthy image. He learned about life, the rigors of the railroad, and the personal sacrifices railroaders make. Much of the time Robert Ludwig accompanied him on these treks, both in the United States and in Latin America. Rose wrote about what it could be like:

Ever ridden a freight train? It's a sobering experience. Ride them for a while and you become part of another world. Where those who couldn't endure the awkwardness or frustration of normal life, or who were on the run, established levels of endurance most of us couldn't imagine.

His explorations suggest a complex personality: artist, adventurer, rebel, and highly independent. When nineteen and twenty years old, he worked for *Trains* magazine at its downtown Milwaukee location. He blazed with talent, creating a painting for a cover and soaking up everything he could learn from David P. Morgan, the magazine's legendary editor from that period. But he couldn't suppress his youthfulness even in the edgy atmosphere of an editorial office. One day he left shoes at home and came barefoot to work. As he emerged from the elevator, he caught the displeasured eye of the magazine's button-down publisher, A. C. Kalmbach, who was not known for casual dress. After service in Viet Nam, Ted Rose did not pick up a camera again.

His photography collection consists of about 4,400 prints and negatives, all black and white. Their quality suggests his artistic impulses, and selections were shown twice during the 1970s in Santa Fe where he lived and worked during his adult life. Now they are being shown more widely, courtesy of his widow, Polly, and the Center.

Mexico in 1960–1961

Right: Engineer and fireman in the cab of National Railways of Mexico MR-7 4-6-2 locomotive no. 2687. It is likely serving on train 237 or 238, a mainline, heavy-duty mixed train that ran between Aguascalientes and Irapuato on a tight schedule.

Below: Two National Railways of Mexico steam locomotives, 2-8-2 no. 2210 and 2-8-0 no. 1414, team up on a freight train approaching the 1.5 percent grade to Zacatecas, elevation 8,075 feet, in central Mexico.

Smoke fills of the summer sky of central Mexico as three locomotives—two up front and one pushing
at the rear—lift a heavy northbound freight train on the National Railways of Mexico's rugged Mexicano
Division (formerly the Mexican Railroad) near Apizaco, about seventy miles east of Mexico City. The rock
formation in the background at far left is Guatlapanga, and the mountain behind it is La Malinche, a
dormant volcano that, at 14,636 feet, is the sixth-highest peak in Mexcio. Photographer Frank Barry, who
lived in Mexico at the time, reports that trains with three locomotives were extremely rare.

United States

Right: Colorado & Southern 2-8-0 locomotive no. 641 leading a short freight train on the railroad's branch between Climax and Leadville, Colorado, in 1960. The C&S used steam on the branch until 1962—long after the rest of the railroad was dieselized—due to the high altitude (Leadville is 10,152 feet).

Below: Duluth, Missabe & Iron Range no. 229, one of the road's massive 2-8-8-4 "Yellowstone" locomotives, leading an iron ore train near Proctor, Minnesota, in 1959.

Above: Chicago, Burlington & Quincy 2-8-2 locomotive no. 4960 leads a passenger excursion through Illinios about 1960.

Left: Graham County Railroad Shay locomotive no. 1925 leads a short freight train at Sweetgum, North Carolina, in the early 1960s.

Significant Images of Railroading

Canadian National 2-8-2 locomotive
no. 3550 on the turntable at the
road's engine terminal in Winnipeg,
Manitoba, in 1959.

Canada

Left: Canadian National turntable operator and 4-8-2 steam locomotive 6075 at the roundhouse in Winnipeg, Manitoba, in 1959.

Below: An eleven-car Canadian Pacific Railway local freight train steams through the prairies behind a 4-6-0 locomotive near Indian Head, Saskatchewan, in 1959.

Fred M. Springer Collection

Wherever Fred Springer went from 1950 until the early 2000s, he seems to have had a camera at the ready to exuberantly document his beloved railroads (especially narrow-gauge lines), his work in the oil industry, and his family. He understood completely the emotional and industrial niches his images filled and, as well, the value of the sizeable collection of railroad timetables and passes that he assembled.

So as he valiantly coped with his final illness, which took his life in 2012 at the age of eighty-three, he made every effort to guarantee that his photographs and memorabilia were bestowed on appropriate institutions and individuals along with sufficient funds for their preservation. He also made sure that the public would have access to his railroad images. Nearly every railroad photographer worries about these problems; too few find solutions before their deaths and fewer still have the financial wherewithal to implement them as Springer did.

Fred Springer (1928–2012) well knew this generally unsatisfactory record for preserving railroad photography and photographers' general lack of means to underwrite preservation of their own work. But he encouraged all donors to provide, to the extent possible, some funding or assistance for preservation and processing of their images and collections. While he treasured the quirks and vagaries of railroading, he also treasured worthwhile images of railroads everywhere, in all guises, and urged their preservation for undertakings of all sorts, ranging from railfan enjoyment, to every form of publication, to serious study of railroad equipment and its taxonomies.

Springer and his wife Dale lived for about thirty years in Salado, Texas, fairly near Temple, a city of 66,000 about 150 miles south of Dallas. Temple was served for decades by the Santa Fe and the Missouri-Kansas-Texas railroads. Springer contributed heavily to the development of Temple's Railroad and Heritage Museum in the Santa Fe depot, and the city named the surrounding park for Springer. He contributed his railroad library and a large timetable and pass collection to the museum, and he personally funded an archivist to catalog the collection and oversee preservation work. (In the museum world, such generosity is just as welcome as it is in the railfan world.) In his backyard at Salado, he built a miniature live-steam railroad whose engines pulled many cars; he supplemented his three steam engines with three electric ones. He also owned a Santa Fe *Super Chief* lounge car that he donated in 2001 to the Arizona Railway Museum in Chandler.

His photographs naturally emphasize his favorite railroads: narrow gauge, especially the 3-foot gauge lines of Colorado including those of the Denver & Rio Grande Western and the Rio Grande Southern, Ecuador's remarkable 3-foot, 6-inch Guayaquil & Quito Railway, and southern Argentina's 2-foot, 5½-inch "Old Patagonia Express," or *La Trochita*, "The Little Gauge." Fred and Dale Springer rode the "Express" four or five times. Springer called the railroad "unbelievable, … 402 kilometers long, the closest thing still running that is a replica of Southern Pacific's narrow gauge in California." He saw similarities between California and Patagonia landscapes and climates. "Both are in quasi-desert areas," he wrote, "and [have] parallel mountain ranges, the Andes in Argentina versus the Sierras in California."

Opposite: Rio Grande Southern "Galloping Goose" no. 4 crossing the Ophir High Trestle near Ophir, Colorado, on August 19, 1950. While color slides comprise the majority of Springer's photography, his black-and-white negatives from the 1950s and 1960s include stunning scenes of Colorado narrow-gauge railroads.

Springer Collection Overview
Gift of Fred and Dale Springer
8,000 B&W negatives
48,000 color slides
1950s to 2000s
All six inhabited continents and especially the southwestern United States, Mexico, and South America

Though his first love was steam locomotives, Springer developed a special fondness for the "Galloping Goose" fleet of home-built railcars of the Rio Grande Southern. His first trip on a Goose out of Ridgway, Colorado, occurred on August 19, 1950 (the date appears on the negative jacket), and was with four family members, including his father, George. Beginning in 1998, Springer served as rear brakeman on Goose no. 5 out of Chama, New Mexico, on the Cumbres & Toltec Scenic Railroad.

Springer's early photography reflected his residency in the Southwest. While born in Washington, DC, he grew up in Houston, went to college at the Missouri School of Mines in Rolla in the southeast quadrant of Missouri, and worked for Mobil Oil Corporation and subsidiary companies in many North American locations. Mobil assigned him to its New York offices for a total of fourteen years in the 1960s through the 1980s and to its Chicago offices for seven years. While working in the Chicago area he lived in Lake Bluff, Illinois, where his three children all were graduated from high school. During those years away from the Southwest, he captured on film several northeastern U.S. lines, some Canadian lines in the maritime provinces, and midwestern U.S. lines.

In retirement, Fred and Dale traveled parts of six continents by train, photographing as they went. They especially reached North and South America and Europe. But they also visited several southern nations in Africa, Syria and Jordan in Asia, plus Australia and New Zealand—not commonly on American railfans' itineraries. He frequently visited Mexico beginning in the 1960s when steam was still operating. Selected images from his store of narrow-gauge lines have appeared in the railfan press and in various books.

Springer's donation to the Center consists of close to 48,000 color slides and 8,000 black-and-white negatives. Significantly, Springer's images do not record rail activity in the major Asian nations—China, Japan, and India. Nevertheless Fred Springer's astonishing, sixty-year odyssey along the world's railroads is an equally astonishing accomplishment, as was his financial generosity that has guaranteed the preservation and availability of these 56,000 images for the edification and pleasure of generations yet to come.

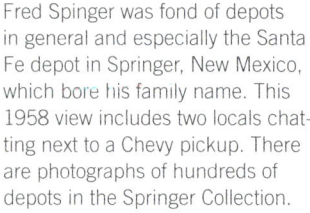

Fred Spinger was fond of depots in general and especially the Santa Fe depot in Springer, New Mexico, which bore his family name. This 1958 view includes two locals chatting next to a Chevy pickup. There are photographs of hundreds of depots in the Springer Collection.

Left: Texas Transportation Company no. 1, a 60-ton steeplecab electric locomotive built by Baldwin in 1917, switches at the Pearl Brewery in San Antonio, Texas, in April 1977. The electric railroad operated from 1897 until the brewery closed in 2001. Springer photographed little-known short line and industrial railroads throughout the U.S. and especially in Texas and neighboring states.

Below: Steam and diesel locomotives switch freight cars on the Angelina & Neches River Railroad in the city of Lufkin, Texas, in 1961.

United States

Right: Santa Fe no. 809, a General Electric C40-8W, leads a mixed freight train through Abo Canyon, New Mexico, on June 29, 1995. Springer continued photographing the contemporary rail scene, in the U.S. as well as abroad, until very close to the end of his life.

Below: Three former Rio Grande 2-8-2 narrow-gauge steam lcomotives out of Chama, New Mexico, lead an eastbound photo charter train up Cumbres Pass on the Cumbres & Toltec Scenic Railroad on July 27, 1996. Springer was very active as a volunteer on the C&TS and photographed it frequently.

Union Pacific 4-8-4 locomotive no.
8444 pulling an excursion train near
Carr, Colorado, on August 21, 1978.
Springer rode and photographed
mainline steam excursions exten-
sively throughout the United States
during his lifetime.

In 1963, following a meet with train no. 110 at Cañelas, National Railways of Mexico train no. 257, pulled by 2-8-0 no. 288, prepares to pull out of a siding to continue its journey on the three-foot-gauge main line.

Fred M. Springer Collection

Mexico

Fred Springer made numerous trips to Mexico between 1963 and 2000, and his photographs from those trips depict nearly four decades of change in the country and its railroads.

Left: Clouds roll above the Sierra Madre Oriental mountain range as a National Railways of Mexico train negotiates the line between Toluca and Saltillo in May 1968.

Below: Burros cross the three-foot-gauge tracks at a village along the National Railways of Mexico line between Puebla and Matamoros in May 1968.

Australia and New Zealand

Right: V/Line commuter passenger train approaching the Melbourne station on March 26, 1997.

Below: New Zealand's *Tranz Alpine* passenger train crossing a viaduct in the Southern Alps on January 17, 1994. The scenic route crosses the South Island via Arthurs Pass.

Fred M. Springer Collection

Europe

An electric-hauled passenger train on Switzerland's Rhaetian Railway crossing the Langwieser Viaduct over the Plessur River valley in August 1998. The viaduct, completed in 1914 and standing 203 feet above the river, is next to Langwies Station of the meter-gauge line from Chur to the resort town of Arosa.

Africa and the Middle East

Right: Beyer-Garratt locomotive no. 608, a 2-8-2+2-8-2 of the 16A class based in Bulawayo, Zimbabwe, on August 2, 1991.

Below: Schoolchildren in Wankie, Zimbabwe, line the fence separating their school yard from the railroad tracks, on August 6, 1991. Wankie is a hub of coal-mining operations, and coal dust and soot cover the ground and permeate the air. The children are drawn to Springer's group of American and European rail photographers.

Above: Two South African Railways Class 7 4-8-0 steam locomotives lead a passenger excursion train across the towering steel bridge over the Malgaarten River on the line between George and Mossel Bay on March 21, 1995.

Left: During his only trip to the Middle East, Springer spent several days photographing railways in Jordan. Here 2-8-2 no. 71 of the Hedjaz Jordan Railway leads a three-car passenger train across a stone arch viaduct, which carries an aquaduct on a lower level. This view is from the outskirts of Amman on July 15, 1991. Two minaret towers in the background are visible Islamic hallmarks of Middle East culture and architecture.

Ecuador's spectacular Guayaquil & Quito Railway was one of Fred Springer's favorites, harkening back to the Colorado narrow-gauge lines that had captivated him as a young man in the United States. In the view above, Baldwin-built 2-8-0 no. 44 leads a four-car train up the Devil's Nose near Alausi in July 1988. In another view (right) from the same trip, a freight train led by Baldwin 2-6-0 no. 11 waits in a siding for railbus no. 92 to pass. Railbuses such as the 92, which were more economical to operate than a short steam-hauled train, provided extensive passenger service across the often harsh and remote terrain of the G&Q.

Fred M. Springer Collection

South America

Left: Railbus M-323 operating over a fog bound mountain pass on the rail line connecting Bolivia and Chile on September 29, 1992.

Below: Double-headed steam train on one of Springer's favorite railroads, the "Old Patagonian Express" or *La Trochita* of the spectacular Argentine region of Patagonia. This view is from near the Esquel end of the line on October 30, 1995.

About the Center

Founded in 1997, the Center for Railroad Photography & Art is a national nonprofit arts and educational organization based in Madison, Wisconsin. As its mission the Center "preserves and presents significant images of railroading, interpreting them in publications, exhibitions, and on the Internet."

The Center conducts its programs in-house and, with the aid of numerous partners, throughout the country, as with a recent collaboration with the Chicago History Museum on the exhibition, "Railroaders: Jack Delano's Homefront Photography," and an accompanying 200-page catalog prepared by the Center. They tell the stories of forty-nine Chicagoland railroad workers during World War II and serve as a prime example of the kind of work that can be created from a significant, well-preserved collection of rail photography. As museum president Gary Johnson said, "Museums with photographic archives, take heed!"

The Center also mounts traveling exhibitions about railroad workers and individual photographers such as O. Winston Link and David Plowden. Venues include Grand Central Terminal, the California State Railroad Museum, and Milwaukee's Grohmann Museum. Support from the North American Railway Foundation (NARF) led to the long-running "Representations of Railroad Work" program. All told, the Center has brought twenty unique exhibitions of railroad photography and art to sixty venues throughout the country.

Efforts to preserve railroad photography and artwork have led to the Center's amassing some 200,000 images, principally the works of the ten collections featured in this summary publication. The Center has conducted many of its preservation activities in concert with the Archives & Special Collections of the Donnelley and Lee Library at Lake Forest College.

Publication of the Center's journal, *Railroad Heritage*, occurs quarterly. Each issue features work by historic and contemporary photographers and artists plus news of developments in the field. With NARF's help, special issues have honored workers, women in railroading, and individual photographers, and have concisely explained railroad history and preservation.

Each spring, the Center hosts its annual Conversations about Photography conference, typically at Lake Forest College, thirty miles north of Chicago. The conference provides a forum for veteran and young photographers alike—as well as artists, historians, editors, and railroaders—to mingle both socially and formally, present and discuss their work, and address photographic and artistic issues. Thanks to the generosity of several conference patrons, the Center recently began offering scholarships to enable young or developing photographers and artists to attend the conference.

The annual John E. Gruber Creative Photography Awards Program recognizes recent work by railroad photographers in the United States and abroad. Named for the Center's principal founder, the awards program includes an exhibition at the California State Railroad Museum and publication in *Railfan & Railroad* magazine.

Internet sites www.railphoto-art.org and www.railroadheritage.org expound on the Center's activities and provide an online image archive with detailed descriptions. The Center maintains many additional online resources at Facebook, Flickr, Twitter, Amazon, Youtube, RailPictures.net, and Trainsmag.com. Follow them to stay abreast of current events and trends in railroad photography and the Center's research and acquisitions.

Tracks of the Kingston Branch near
Lake Wakatipu on New Zealand's
South Island, January 22, 1994.
Fred M. Springer